48 Hours in

Sydney

Contents

▮ SCHOLASTIC

Published in the UK by
Scholastic Education, 2024
Scholastic Distribution Centre, Bosworth Avenue,
Tournament Fields, Warwick, CV34 6UQ
Scholastic Ireland, 89E Lagan Road, Dublin
Industrial Estate, Glasnevin, Dublin, D11 HP5F

SCHOLASTIC and associated logos are
trademarks and/or registered trademarks of
Scholastic Inc.
www.scholastic.co.uk

© 2024 Scholastic

1 2 3 4 5 6 7 8 9   4 5 6 7 8 9 0 1 2 3

Printed by Ashford Colour Press

This book is made of materials from
well-managed, FSC®-certified forests
and other controlled sources.

MIX
Paper from
responsible sources
FSC
www.fsc.org   FSC® C011748

A CIP catalogue record for this book is available
from the British Library.

ISBN 978-0702-32735-3

Author
Rachel Russ

Editorial team
Rachel Morgan, Vicki Yates, Abbie Rushton,
Alison Gilbert

Design team
Dipa Mistry, Andrea Lewis and We Are Grace

Photographs
Cover f11/Shutterstock
p4–5 Taras Vyshnya/Shutterstock
p6–7 bbofdon/Shutterstock
p8–9 pptara/Shutterstock
p10–11 Adwo/Shutterstock
p11 (artist) Pressmaster/Shutterstock
p12–13 f11photo/Shutterstock
p14 narvikk/iStock
p15 sw_photo/Shutterstock
p16–17 katharina13/iStock
p17 (grass tree) alybaba/Shutterstock
p18 cherry-hai/Shutterstock
p19 Sudarat Bomkunthod/iStock
p20 Neale Cousland/Shutterstock
p21 (girl and ferris wheel) mihailomilovanovic/
iStock
p21 (night view of Sydney) Jacob Marsh/
Shutterstock
p22–23 pisaphotography/Shutterstock

Illustrations
p1 (flag) Anton Shahrai/Shutterstock
p6, 8, 10, 12, 15, 16, 18, 19, 21 (map)
Bardocz Peter/Shutterstock
p6, 8, 10, 12, 15, 16, 18, 19, 21 (map pointer)
nice17/Shutterstock

How to use this book

This book practises these letters and letter sounds:

ea (as in 'great')	ere (as in 'here')	dge (as in 'bridge')
ge (as in 'large')	y (as in 'crystal')	ti (as in 'action')
our (as in 'tourists')	ore (as in 'more')	

Here are some of the words in the book that use the sounds above:

Sydney   break   tour   range   collection

edge   explore

These are the key words in the text:

**hours   of   beautiful   to   two   one
the   are   into   eye   any**

Before reading

- Read the title and look at the cover. Discuss what the book might be about.

During reading

- If necessary, sound out and then blend the sounds to read the word: b-r-ea-k-i-ng, breaking.
- Pause every so often to talk about the information.

After reading

- Talk about what has been read.
- Use the index on page 24 to select any pages to revisit

Sydney is a city that is full of surprises. It has beautiful beaches, iconic landmarks and delicious food. Sydney has so much to offer tourists.

This action-packed two-day plan explains how you could have a weekend break exploring one of the most exciting cities in the world.

Day 1

9am

After breakfast, climb the striking Sydney Harbour Bridge. It's great to see the city from the top.

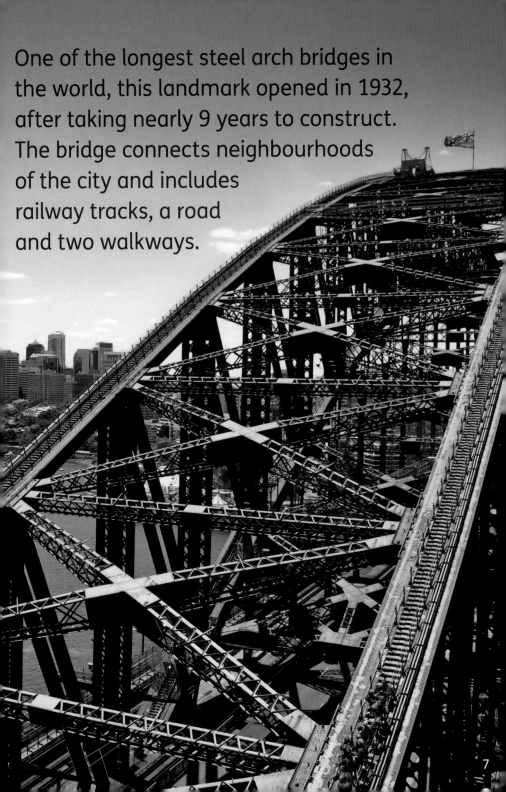

One of the longest steel arch bridges in the world, this landmark opened in 1932, after taking nearly 9 years to construct. The bridge connects neighbourhoods of the city and includes railway tracks, a road and two walkways.

12pm 🕛

For lunch, grab some delicious takeaway food from the shops nearby. Then take your picnic with you on a ferry tour. It offers another amazing chance to enjoy the sensational Sydney skyline, and you can relax and enjoy your lunch at the same time.

The tour includes a talk to tell you all about Sydney's history and famous landmarks.

When you are back on dry land, pop into the MCA – an art gallery with a treasure trove of artworks.

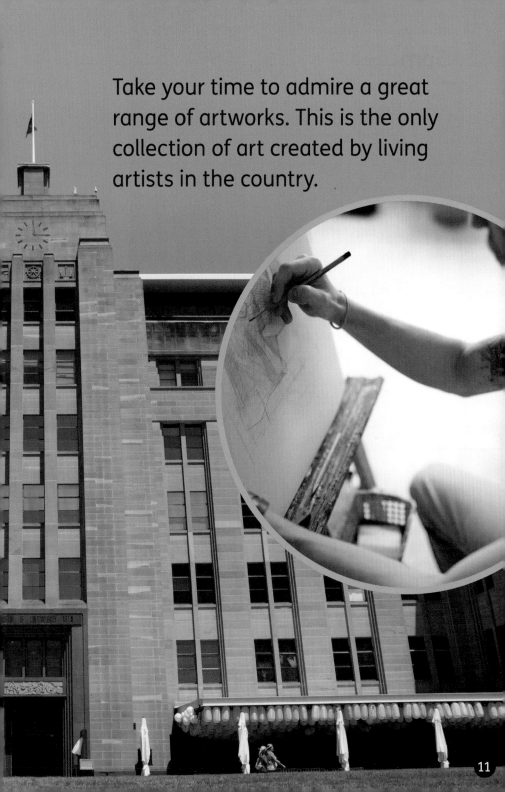

Take your time to admire a great range of artworks. This is the only collection of art created by living artists in the country.

5pm

Don't miss one of the most well-known landmarks in Sydney – the Opera House. With its distinctive white sail-like shapes, it is a spectacular sight.

Soak up the atmosphere and have dinner overlooking the harbour as the sun sets. Then see a performance at the Opera House.

Day 2

Start the day with a healthy breakfast at Bondi Beach, beside the breaking waves. From here, you can stroll along the shore.

Well known for its crystal-clear water, crescent shape and white sand, Bondi is a perfect spot to try surfing.

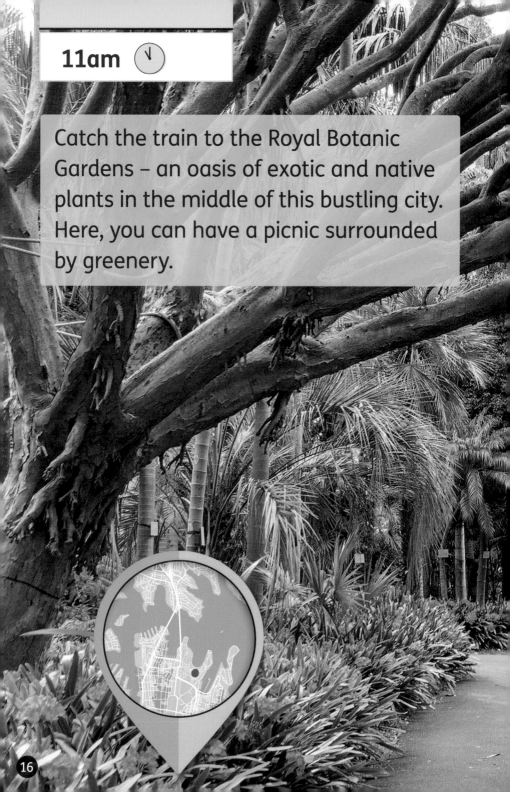

11am

Catch the train to the Royal Botanic Gardens – an oasis of exotic and native plants in the middle of this bustling city. Here, you can have a picnic surrounded by greenery.

You'll see a range of plants here, like grass trees which are only found in this country. They are not grass or trees, but are related to lilies!

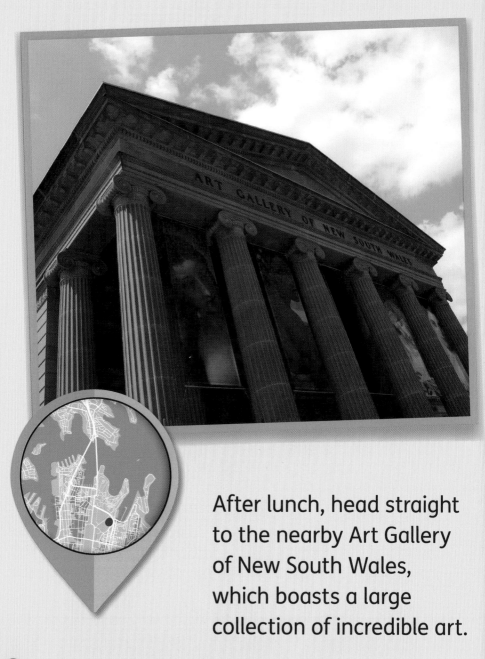

After lunch, head straight to the nearby Art Gallery of New South Wales, which boasts a large collection of incredible art.

3pm

Head up the Sydney Tower Eye for a special outlook across the city. It might feel strange close to the edge!

If you have any energy left, catch a ferry to this amusement park, which is full of attractions. Before you go in, grab a photo beside the iconic smiling face entrance.

After all that activity, you'll be ready for dinner. Stop to eat near the amusement park for a great perspective of the skyline from across the water.

Phew! You'll deserve a rest after an action-packed couple of days.

There is so much more to explore in this exceptional city – you'll wish you had more time!

Index